About the Author

Iraqian-born, Parisian-based, rode the winged horse of the rebellious sixties with a flower in his hand to stab his silhouette with, Abdul Kader El-Janabi set off, at the beginning of 1970, for London looking for the fog which, through American movies, represented for him the veil between an Orient of certitude and an occident of doubt. To write poetry then was to perforate this veil in order to create new poetic correspondences. A whole world of a voluntary exile showed him the need to go beyond dualities and simple contradictions.

He founded in Paris, in 1973, *Le Désir Libertaire*, the first surrealist Arabic review, banned in the Arab world for its critical approach to social and religious issues. But his involvement in surrealism at the time was in no way to poke around in the linen closet of surrealism's obsolete inventions, but a real attachment to Breton's theoretical mind behind the poem. For he knew that to become effective surrealist was first to outdistance the repetitive, then to be ready to doubt even the ideals that our founding fathers have struggled for.

Author of many collections of poetry and essays, a translator into Arabic of many American and European poets such as Paul Celan, René Daumal, Joyce Mansour, William Carlos Williams and recently an international anthology of prose poem, Abdul Kader El-Janabi has also published into French many anthologies of modern Arabic poetry.

Here is a selection of poems and autobiographical pieces of a poet so obsessed with meaning and its relation to image, that he's not entirely wrong in describing himself in one of his early poems as a 'tiger of languages in a jungle of dictionaries'.

A HORSEBACK AFTERNOON
POEMS WRITTEN IN AND OUT OF SURREALISM
1975 TO THE HORIZON 2015

Abdul Kadeer El-Janabi

brokensleepbooks.com

ISBN: 978-1-915079-64-0

Cover art by John Welson: *Season's Song Sung* (2019)

Page 1 art by John Welson: *Sun Finger* (2022)

Cover designed by Aaron Kent

Edited and typeset by Aaron Kent

WALES: CORNWALL:
Broken Sleep Books   Broken Sleep Books
Rhydwen,   Fair View
Talgarreg,   St Georges Road
Ceredigion   Cornwall
SA44 4HB   PL26 7YH

Galloping spirits, collage (1979)
Abdul Kader El-Janabi

Oedipus act, collage (1988)
Abdul Kader El-Janabi

Contents

Hence

The poet's childlike brain, collage (1986)
Abdul Kader El-Janabi

Travelling

It's time to wait for the rain to fall. I like its sound against the window, the drops on the timbre are softer than the wind of the dead. Everything is in its place. Descartes, a pint of pale ale and *The air that I breathe...* by the Hollies. Here I am, alone in this corner of the world, nestled in a sweet harmony; nobody can feign better than the poets. I am sitting far from the present, near the threshold of the eclipse where nostalgia takes shape and animates the landscape: the autumn, which illuminates my childhood with its warm and coppery colors, mixes with shy shadows. Everything is calm, an irregular silence dominates the waves, I feel that the universe is what it is, beings are not matters, but rather particles. In the void, the world is mute, tiny like a flower without a future. Even now I am still the child of hope in search of adventure, yet I am afraid of the phantoms hiding in the waters. Once, running along the river's shore to catch a fish, I fell and almost drowned. My mother often recounted this incident, saying that angels came to my rescue. Since that day, a curious shadow hovers at the bleachers of my unconscious, like the clock that I broke because of its ticking. Our district was always bathed in a subdued light conducive to the reverie, a chiaroscuro of myths. There were discreet places, attractive, that could be considered easily as part of an invisible world, like this abandoned garden around which I liked to wander with other children, while evening was falling dimly on earth which stretches out for insects. We could feel a wind pushing millions of invisible lives into this garden, tiny beings suspended in the air, twirling in the muggy currents, among them ideas leap from one mind to another. In that moment, we scurried away running for our life towards the flabby roofs of our secrets. It was a long time ago. I was ten years old: "You see," said my mother, "the night is wicked, it often dances with the dead, then it eats them like weeds... You can play while it's light." Since then, at every eclipse, I feel a cold sweat. As a matter of fact, I have since built, a special relationship with the night and its shades in the mind. I went out one morning and walked aimlessly; in a bookshop stall I noticed a young poet's collection of poems with a new tone, but the edition was beyond my meagre means. Instead, my choice was then Dashiell Hammett's *The Glass Key*. For prose costs less than verse, and the words are shelved in bulk, but those of poetry are sold in detail, perhaps because they have no country or origin. Contrary to the prose, poetry does not follow any trace. Poetry is a wing of no bird. Prose feeds on fluid ideas. Between the night table and the asphalt of the day, only a leaf allows the intellect to stand on its feet. For what falls from the trees of the countryside hides a distance of humility where the eyebrows of the survivors, point for the spirits to clean the ground while waiting for their chapter to end. Whereas the ideas, in my head, are shifting and turning on themselves, the streets, stone by stone, collect my steps. I riffled through the book and I remembered this sentence, I read once in a review, which gave me food for thought: *when the glass key breaks as it enters the lock, the character still doesn't know what will happen to him; but he knows that there is no turning back, that he has become the plaything of fate, that his struggles will be in vain and that hope is now, at best, an illusion...*

I see prose walking in time through the universe, up to the skyline in a continuous flow between cycles and evolutions. Yet in the memories evoked, the sentences, gluttons for punishment, are like souvenir that amplify their surface, not to imitate it, but to tear it apart. Shaking with shivers and thinking of the multiple sunsets, I took the first street on the left where there is a big postcard bazaar: sepia colors, dusty photos, derelict places, carnival of the past captured freely, all this release syntax from grammatical obligations. Demystifying the rhetoric, the implicit words of the poet direct the vision, an image of an experience, to the octave of the intellect. Thus, he accustoms himself to see both the verticality of the written word and the horizon caught by the reader. Luckily the socialite is a pig wading in its trough! No metaphor enhances its taste. In every spontaneous memory, there is a prose free of genres, subtext of any notion, a narrative in the form of a three-sided mirror, searching the interior for stray moments. It manifests itself abruptly like a crack in the dam, in a sequence of observations representing the movements of the eyes, forward, backward, sideways. Yes, find a high-flying prose and be its outpouring, its instant. It alone can reach the heights of your vision, so high that it can see your name written on the door of paradise, and on the sole condition that it may fortify each word causing the language to alight into rays. This is the mystery of the poet's innominate prose, of his chestnut-shaped visions that spread without reason until they match our desires. It is a prose where the words harbor the disorder of novelty. The swaying shadow is no longer there, the light wins the space and its bright scent unfolds in the open air. The poetic is its own nightmare, as the word is its own bubble. Here are the realms of the poet's morning of mechanizations, an imaginary eruption, the point of view at the center of the subject, molten despair covering the end of the tunnel. It expresses as much as it tells, the word is for it one and indivisible. For us, we poets, the technical means are not the mental-decor of the whole, but in what remains free of such a duality, between the brass (prose) and the marble (poetry), such the exposure of a past in awakening. When the naked prose gives itself to the poet's language, ghostly ideas slip into the complexities of the narrative under the cautious eye of the words. I sit near my window, in the middle of the universe, without clock or rules, at the point where the arrows cross the mind. The world was gone a long time ago. There is a dissonance in the field where the line is a foreshadow. Bend over to pick-up the moon.

—Abdul Kader El Janabi
December 2021

That smell of writing

Bildung

Here is my share of sand:
A purple soul
Born in the desert
Sheltered in a tent
They removed my foreskin
They showed me my totemic ancestor
Picturesque vestiges without redemption
They taught me what is guts
What is ink
Granted me the Scripture
Let me thieve through medieval nights
Holding moon against sun
Hitting on a solution.

When the day of Reason broke
They brought me a camel
- the prophet's mount -
Sent me to work amidst the debris
Splintering mirrors of otherness
In the hope of being attuned to that very theorization
And before falling asleep
They advised me not to dream of perfection
It's lagging behind
They told me
"Decay is in the present
Tomorrow is also decay
Everything will fall apart
Dust is master of all"

They will be back before the light

Those whose word has the shape of death,
Those taken as legislators of the world.
To whom the will was given them
That may know the delights of surrender.
Those, audiles, then visionaries,
Whose imagination stares down over man
When the spirit groans in the night,
In them the passion of blood ignites
Like a *child in love with maps and stamps.*
These are the conquerors of the past.
They return, one, and by one,
Figures then ghosts
In verse and prose
With fear as half-awakened
As if the snow should hesitate
And murmur in the wind.
They murmur in their sleep:
O logos, take us with you *to the door we never opened.*
Cursed in their own tongue,
They stand naked without a fig leaf.
The serpent feeds them the evils of the tree of knowledge.
They bow their necks,
With hatchets sunk into their skulls
To rip the god out of the machine.
Over there, the one whose memory reveals to us
All that it entails...
And in here, is the one who wanders
like a cloud without rain.
Already like a boat roaring with joy,
They leave our shadows adrift over time.
Nowhere is their Eden
Is there nowhere more dreamed of than poems?
But they have, for an answer, only the pangs of the day

And the hazards of the night,
The symbols and their shining
Utopias clothed in ashes
The silence buried under the cries of the snow
Where the noble soul purifies itself...
Let them speak the language of numbers
Let them organize themselves in luminous ranks to maintain the distance,
Let them blow the spirit into the ashes of the earth,
However far from crossing the uterine threshold.
For they are *half-man and half-star*
Like a widow's bird
Or an old horse. And yet
They stop, once again, at the edge of the horizon
Then leave one more.
From the holes in their pockets
Birds and mists escape.
Weary, they give in to the journey
Wherever the ships doze.
They deceive their absence
And, with their eyes, devour heavenly bodies.
They have been born since the dawn...
And they disappear sooner or later
In the gloom of time
Overtaken by a thirst for the poem.
They die young
No matter how old they seem.
The centuries to come are already shown to them.
A reverence, a hair
        And a rill of ire
In the depths of their eyes.

How small they are in the light of day!
And how great they are in memory's eyes!

History always wants to refer me to you, Andre Breton

1

These lines are dedicated to the bandits of the windy city

André Breton,
Windows are open
And your becoming is eyed by their curtains.

From under the blanket of unapplied thought
I see you holding a dream
Curved between your hands
A phoenix smeared with blond haze rises up
And gives you a sultry look
For you are handsome like "a militant swan"
Whose tongue is wading into my enemy's mouth.

Indications of flames you smile
Foresights which permit
Civilizations fusion with celestial bodies
Streets to pile in mobile corpses
And flowers to bleed the four corners of the air.

There is no bird curious to fornicate a wood
The old-timers are of no consequence.

To furbish their sobered call
They kneaded the tongues of a horizontal insomnia
They are priest-ridden dogs
The needle of death is their phallic symbol
And I should say
You have to go down the paper
Loaded with a growling anguish
To be hurled on the bedrooms of their visions.
 But you come to me never with what they know.

For I see you a woodfire butterfly
Cleaving cascades of knowledge
A blazing running waters
Whose depth is a shape of elsewhere
An epicurean domain engraved on the stone of flesh
With fingers comparable
To the interior convulsions of uneven sounds
Then I see you "touching only the heart of things"
And mossy vibration
As a limpid nightfall
Tiptoes in my wide-awake sleep.

You "hold the thread"
And I still see a curious childhood
Stronger than death
Weaving invisible sands.

Implanted in the shores of sleepless mirrors
Where the gesture of insurrections
Sings its reincarnation.

The poem is a being
And history - the hive of ironies - is in no hurry
To see that a windy city
Is reserved
For your springs.

2

At the bottom of the dream, reality awaits me.

I see the ugliness of our time translating
An action of thought in mere graffiti on a dubious wall
I see no entrance to imagination not guarded
By the very ones who lack imagination
I see a vagabond,
After having rested bleeding,
Lying like a truth and hoping only to sleep
I see the daylight, though avid for seducing the virginity
Of the night, squashing its shadows
Seeking a point of reference.

On my way to the unknown
I see birds delivering sermons to certain frogs!

It is nightfall.
My mouth smokes a long scream, while slipping away
Into a falling silence.

On my way to the unknown
I am alone, digging a grain of thought
Immersed in me. I flurry, I shift the site
Of my whereabouts trying to perceive the right direction.
But deep in the leaping heart of an ashen humanity
My eyes give ground.

On my way to the unknown
I see neither the commonplace
Nor sign of phalanstery
I capture from afar, a tangible fact which reveals
A feverish principality blazing a trail
Of an experimental earthly creation.

On my way to the unknown
I only hope to retain enough mettle to go the whole way
To reach the festive courtyard of the womb
And dance in its embrace.
For a mirror in the dark
Provides more than just a reflection,
It exemplifies the kind of attention posterity should have.

3

For pierre peuchmaurd

We were children in search of happiness
Happiness in search of children
We were antithesis of a world
Off light
A mountain without slope
We were a golden fleece
The mob couldn't reach
We were the voice
And the poem
The morning
And the light
The head
And the practice before the game
We were the white-haired revolver
In the worker's hand
While the bullet
Was down there
In the heart
Fumbling
Between the lines
For words.

We were howling
Like a hurricane wind
To settle the score
That history will glare
From the exquisite corpse
And lean
On our graveyard.

Anima

A man heard a voice coming from across the river. *He threw off his clothes and swam across the river* towards all that is forgotten. The voice had gone by the time he landed. He stood there, lulled by the rolling of the landscape's living waters, perceiving the echo that rose like a breath from the depths of his throat.

The grace of paradox

In the mid-sixties, on a visit to the American Library in Baghdad, I picked up a book I have forgotten its title. Upon reading it, I realized that the philosopher is one who stabilizes words, they become confined, dedicated to straightforward denotation. Since the poet is a disturber, his words in contrast modify one another, violating their lexical meaning! from that time, I sought the excitement in the calm; the sacred in the profane and so on. I started to investigate the field of contradictions, far from the ocean of metaphors.

A dream

One day I went for a walk-through Al-Saray souk, Baghdad's old bazaar. In the back of a shop stifling with dust, a painting caught my eye:

On a secluded beach,
Shredded limbs,
          An empty chair,
            A weary shell!

It was apparently a portrait of a half-veiled woman lying on the sand and rubbing her navel with her slender fingers.
I looked at it more closely. I found that in the face of her distress, the diaphanous breast flooded with blaspheme, the flesh seemed so vile that the dust lost its importance.

Sepia

In the homeland
In the family photo
The mother in her old dress
In a room
Around a table
Before the big departure
Breastfeeds the child
The father counts his coins.
Rags on a chair
A broom against a bare wall
In the homeland
Before the debacle
In the family photo.
Time passed like a dream

Scene of war

What can I hope for
      In these times of war?
No chance of coming back.
I must go up to the periphery,
     To the north of the battle
             Where I'll be safe for tonight.

Form and content

Night has neither ghosts nor angels... It is just odious darkness. In the kingdom of the earth, it extends its roots by seas and mountains. Starlit, it advances above the universe. Like a knight, it stalks the unseen, where the eye begins. When the light sleeps in the whiteness of the earth, it does so with the prisoners who guard the well, under which truth is cast. The shadow, in its spiral funeral, opens the night's distracted eyes because all the demons use it as a post office. In the night of the mind, the candle never goes out. The dark gleams.

Writing in the head

Suddenly, a room emerges like a bull's-eye, three-square meters in size, with its bed, its table and corners… It's barely a room, yet it has a blurred window from which I enter slowly to bury the jailer of my solitudes. The muezzin of metaphor pierces my eardrum. He draws the intellect down to words, absorbent, waded and unexploitable; they reconstruct their works with sparks escaping from the blows of an adze out of the blue. Everything hovers towards grace, but the word towards what flies in its vault.

Sequence

In the dark corridor of meaning words digress, leaving what was revealed to the mind suspended in the lurch. Writing unites you with the womb. It helps you to grip the beyond. No smoke of there-to-be. Just becoming. At the end of the night, a tremor of ideas scatters the leaves and transforms the song of the useless into a ritual of flashes where blasphemers meet and then vanish.

Old images are dead

We who have the strength to stand
We are still fixing the sap of artifice
And planting our poems in the grass,
We should not despair about horizon.
There will always be a new and grand hour
To tease rivers and skyscrapers,
To dip our feathers in the blood of the goddesses
So that our intelligence escapes
From its solitude and lies under the trees!
We feel the need to melt into petrified tears,
To meet our eons,
To love and dream
    Of the unity of word and body
        To offer wonders
           And say goodbye to our ghosts.

A horseback afternoon

I was afraid of falling dead all of a sudden, just like that. But this thought was quickly abandoned, and I began to worry: what had happened to my father, why is he late, we were supposed to meet here in front of the windows of the Orosdiback galleries: he promised to buy me a suit. For tomorrow is the first day of the Eid; I must put on new clothes in order to earn everyone's respect - especially of the girl I've been after for a month. What had happened to him? Half an hour has already passed. The second hand of the watch runs on, doubling the intensity of my worries. People come in and out, in perpetual motion. I turned left and right, there was no trace of my old man. I wonder if, once again, he had wandered into the vineyards of the Lord. A large hourglass, displayed in the window, captivated my gaze as the silica flowed into lower bulb, down to the last grain. I saw that the department stores close early, as they did every holiday evening. Here is the last customer just leaving, the curtains are falling and the lights abandoned me one by one. Darkness enveloped me and the echo of my footsteps was the only thing that resounded in my head all the way home. When I arrived, I went to my room, and to my surprise, I saw a gray suit on my bed, along with a sky-blue shirt and a banknote to spend! In my sleep, I saw myself in a carriage with a girl on the way to Roxy cinema which was showing a Marlon Brando's film A Street car named desire.

Dream

… then the hero entered the forest. He stopped under the apple tree mentioned in the fables. A dove was about to land on one of its branches when a furious wind blew accompanied by nasty rain. The hero noticed that the numbers and letters were running out of the book of shadows as soon as the wide eyes of the eternal one, hidden in the foliage, were blinking. Mingled with the rustling of a flock of birds through the trees, the hours passed, like the kidnappings in past times. The figure of a small winged girl dressed as a huntress, drew him to a pond where the ancient gods once came to drink. He realized that he had penetrated too far into the swarthiness in which the forest was enclosed. The exit could already be seen pointing beyond the supernova buried in the mud of the firmament. In the heart of this substance in gestation, he felt in his heels the space loaded with its angry elements and its effigies which have subterranean echoes. He delved into memories. Past and future intertwined at the foot of the present. Heaven and earth huddled against one another. A struggle for metamorphoses! And suddenly the hero's right eye reddened the whole scene, at the moment his left eye burst into sparks which set the fire to the undergrowth in a painting hanging on the wall of my childhood.

End of the class

At noon, light poured into the amphitheater. An unrecognized philosopher was listening for the slightest whisper. The students in the bleachers, head in the clouds as they went through each sentence, each word. In their minds, a world was awakening. They fell into a mad meditation. The philosopher rushed to the blackboard where words were already springing from the blue chalk: *The whole is false*, almost true. And all of a sudden, silence clashed with a pack of wolves!

Supreme Region

How many times have I awoken
From a deep sleep,
Without remembering
A snatch of a dream.

I fall asleep beside a fairy
On the floor of the constellation
Long before the dawn
In a bed of dead leaves.

Above the city
Angels in sleeveless dresses
        Disjointed
Came face to face
  With the guardians of the moon.

I hear the whisper of the tree of paradise
In whose shade the mystics
Strive to spin the verses of ecstasy
From their authorized intoxication.

I see the woman without a veil
    Entering my poem
     And follow the ink to the trace,
     To the glory of stars,
Nailed on the gate that gives access to the earth.

Oracle

Since the beheading of Orpheus
The blood of the poets
Is still pouring out
     Up to the door of the poem!

Silence

Once again:
Nightless,
        Stars,
         Without hope,
Thick as a fog,
    Invade,
        Endlessly,
The clock of my life!

All comes to harmony

We need the white tips of existence
To light the invisible door,
The corporal time that wraps us,
The formlessness of our own.
The loneliness that grows with every din,
And the window curtain we lower
Every time we're together.

Visit

A half-awake night owl comes from afar,
A notebook in one hand
A pen in the other
And in his looks,
Close to the eyelids,
A storm of words!

Larger than the seasons

On its asphalt axis,
Our city sleeps in peace.
The streets in multicolored orbs,
The houses,
        Feet in the water,
And the inhabitants going like arrows
Towards the breaking day of their misery!
This is the war-torn climate of the seasons.

Like the sea, life retreats
And clouds of lace stand by the sky.

A unique opportunity
That may the earth be sweeter than its flowers!

The land of our farewell,
        Where the storm
        Does not tear up the fragile grass,
But it cuts down the large trees,
Shattering the heritage of the street light
And keeps the dwelling boundless!

Permanence of transience

In the forest of nowhere,
Among the trees of the countryside,
A surface of humility hides
So that the brows of the survivors
Soften while waiting for
The dead to clean the ground
And the chapter to be closed.

Theory is its nightmare
As the word is its ball.

Since it is so late

The beings of sky are sleeping
    In the vast bed of the centuries.
Baghdad sleeps on the stream of memories,
Without hope,
    Without a well,
      A mere river emptied of its boats
        Like a mirror without reflection.

At night the lamps take their breath
And lift the seeds of darkness,
Dispersed by a wind of appearance.

The howl of the Garden of Eden,
    So precious,
Is the only founding sound
In this dialectic between body and love,
    And a world that thinks in symbols.

The embrace is the fullness of a nearby paradise.
The djinns are already at work,
    Setting out the stage.

In Surrealism's name

Once again,
From colored eyelids
        To the curve of the lashes,
Our blissful History awakens
whole series of conquests,
    Illuminating every page of the annals,
Tales of all the deeds and gestures
    In the corridor of fulfilled times.

History,
With banners unfurled,
     Crawling through the ages,
    Evocative steam,
Nuanced, twisted and greedy,
      Guardian of our poems,
Feeding the ants,
     Sent like a thousand signs
        Off the dunes,
Modeling our statue of glory
    At the end of the line.

In the past, people hurried for the oracles,
History kept a gap
Leaving everything running in a field.
To flicker in their hearts; a heal.

 History is a book,
    Foaming from page to page,
Soaked our dreams in appendices and opposites,
While we hid in its folds.

And yet

We and History,
      Sheep and the green grass of the remnants,
Are clinging together for better or for worse.

Boats... on the water...

Sometimes clouds
    And lighthouses,
        Sometimes semaphores
           On a boulevard,
Or
    Luminous moment
        Of a mirage
           Orphaned by the gaze.

Portrait of Ramses Younane

The son of Miniah
Has triggered his rebellion
To slow the representation
And the eye takes a fly
Towards the white lines of the interrupted word
        Of the centuries.

The man has stretched out
On the ridge of the void
When space coloured his palette
And lost forms exploded
    In improbable shaded.

What would the clocks of Cairo think
If not of the cries of men,
Of the crumbs of sadness,
And of the distance of doves
 At the end of sight.

The son of Miniah
Untouchable solitaire
Loaded with images
Has traded his role
As a bystander
And leapt into the heart of things
Leaving to the horizon
Traces to nibble
To History an underpass,
To the meaningless a chance to redeem itself
To painting the infancy of the eve.

Thrown into the fray

Trailing the collective dream
On the canvas of the future.

Artificial paradise

My nights with the surrealists,
Without beginning, middle or end,
Extend along the instant.
They pass like Danae.
The eyebrows painted pink
Between the *conspiratorial sheets* of the street
      And the laughter of id.
They whisper love
    In front of the cracks of a debacle.

Their long wings
Carry me to the Olympus of wonder.
Climbing the mount of riots,
And the exquisite corpse
    To drink the wine of the game,
      From the vase of cry!

Aurora

With an old-fashioned metaphor
I fire up images
To warm the hut.

The forest, black widow,
Depressing with its hectic mysteries,
Tying its web
To the door of the soul.

Murderers are baffled.
The world is so near its end
That the skin of its grief
Shrinks
When its creator overwhelms it with fables.

The forerunner

He too,
Sleeps, sleeps in the stones,
The vivid discovery digs at him.
And prompts him to start all over again!
He wakes in a glass cage,
Without reference,
He follows the idle progress from the seventh heaven,
Carried like a leaf by the north wind,
 Like a tree far from the plains
An angel reborn by his own ray of light.
He no longer knows how to cultivate his garden.
He walks on the splendor of yore,
Fever is his cloak.
He aims his bow and fires a different arrow,
He sizzles, gestures, drifts...
He ignores what binds him to the unfinishable poem,
An epigone of anguish,
The acquired corpse of the narrative.
He dreams of clocks and rain.
His city of cellos
And the corners of his lips
Radiate discreet interpretations of the Book
Through which the faithful are always snaking.

In the depths of the poem

I have a plethora of beginnings
Stretched from the first dawn
To the last sunset,
From suspended odes
To the skimmed asphalt of the canvas,
Material for harlequin,
That mixes chimeras with ruins,
Inflating the liabilities of history.

Despite the rain, the notch,
And the scattered anxieties on the sand,
Beginnings redraw the horizon,
Dissipating like a wandering mist.

I watch then for the spring's burst
In the naked windows of language.
I collect the ephemera
And forget the fanfares.

Beginnings that always lay in wait
At the end of the road.
One has to venerate them
So that, from nocturnal obligation,
Decadence is freed.

Cinema

I was reading The Thousand and One Nights.
I was fifteen years old.
When I came to rub Aladdin's lamp,
It was empty.

Instead, I took flight
On a film,
    Arching through the sky
In pursuit of the vamps!

The fall

It is the day of the ascension.
The soul falls from the fifth floor
      To the sixth
To settle its accounts
With the beyond.

Towards the hidden

The back and forth of a spirit,
Imitated by the branches of the past,
Mix movement with the opaqueness
        Of a pencil dancing on a book
Falling from the hair of a tired sky.
Soon no more.
All at deadlock,
In a despairing estuary of silence.

Limits of analogy

The man,
    Key to the enigma authority,
Is free to progress
    In the exclamation of his dialectic
After the death of the constant.

He is parallel to nakedness
    Defined through his tall chestnut-tree.

To overcome and resurface,
There is no other calculation
On the night bed than the storm,
    In its immediacy.

Thinking of the edge of the curve,
The strangeness of leisure
    Is the ambush
        Itself.

The man,
    A torrent of reflection,
Keeps the demons of the mirror warm.

Ode

O muse, who hides
Under my pen,
Twirling between lines,
I am not another,
  But a plain mirror effect,
A chalice of descending gazes!

Deep

I waited.
I saw nothing pass.
Only splinters thrown in all directions,
        Without any result.
A vestige of thoughts
    Amidst the din!

A Sufi's intoxicated peregrination

He falls asleep.
He dreams.
He catches the hint.
He listens to heaven whispering.
He awakens a memory.
He fills his heart, love and tears.
He walks.
He edges his universe with the alphabet.
He yawns.
He walks again.
He bathes in an infinite light.
He closes.
He spots his ego annihilated in a cave,
In union with Him.

He escapes,
Whirling in the dunes, to be safe.
He gazes at his spirit.
    It's a ghost.
He drops dead.

The vision
        got lost
In the Sufi's head.

From bed to void

The poets leave tomorrow
With their machines,
Lace the word with the throat,
The mouth with silence,
Exalting the saliva to drip
And the tongue to lick the ink
     Still wet
Of yesterday's poem.

Tomorrow when the day bristles,
The cycle, for our happiness
      Or our torment,
Will repeat signals
And sleep will push down the gate.

Tomorrow,
     Hell knows where,
There will be
     No poets, no poems, no melodies,
Only readers
       Hunting for monologue of a dream,
After words in search of words.

Martyr

Under the glow
        Of the deft moon,
                The river
        Runs impulsively
As if the veils of the drowned
Were a cover-up!

Stance in the desert

For Serge Guilbaut

Upon the ground of knowing
Our masters lie asleep
Heaping in their own dreams
References upon references
To the point of making
The perched birds of the brain
Fly from the skull of the book
Towards a groove
Open in their picture of the past.

They have to make a halt
Between a camel and an airplane
To dig out the lines of continuity
And to flash them up
     Into the palms of our hands.

Translation

While the tongues were licking
      The Tower of Babel,
I was enjoying eating Ishtar's curls
         In their crescent form.

Innocence

I have never seen a mermaid.

The sea on the screen
Has the scent
Of the first streets.
It's agile,
    Silent,
        Slithering like a snake
        Gliding towards its nest.

In its ripples
    Shine
The abscesses of the sun.

Theorem

It is an enameled night
    With a protective darkness.
I alone, on the esplanade of the alchemist,
    Follow its slow streak of light.

Where is Bacchus to transform
    The angels,
        The suspended figures of healing,
Into drunken beggars
    Into wandering musicians marking the rhythm?

I walk alone.
I see in the broken dark
        In a crystal bowl,
    A great fire...
Is it sunshine or illumination?

The nimbus shoots off...

Disjecta membra

For John Welson

There is an egg broken into a well-oiled tongue
A shy horse flirting with the idea
An enclosure of dancing forks and peaceful guns
A hand which rocks the cradle without ruling the world

There is Today a mouse, Tomorrow a man,
Workers' synchronized sound-dream
A memory wounded by a wise saw;
The silver of a jazzman
Crammed with piano-keys sepia times.

There is also a John Welson
To broadcast the seeds of our being there.

Flowing from the unknown

I stroll on the sidewalks of red-handed lips:
A revolving father mingles with
A laconic flare.

Out of the cave

What a point of time
To shriek a warning
To send a shiver down the sand
To grieve for the camel, they shot down.

Abolished love

During love
      Our hearts hang on the wall.
A lifetime of setbacks
For a new loyalty.

During love
We change course,
    Like seabirds,
    And consume in sweat
      All our other desires.

Cogito

My friend is never the same
She carries the world in her hair,
She crushes the anguish of noon
With her memory hoof.

As a horse of the first battle,
She is a stranger to red roses.
Lakes flow from her fingers.
Between her glances
  The sky, the glade
And the bushy undergrowth of the family
        Is discovered.

Sublimation

A poem fell from the sky. I picked it up, cleaned it and pocketed it. I walked for ages. Then I sat on the next bench that I came across. I pulled out of my pocket what I thought was a poem. It was in fact a shopping list with no name, no address... It may have been written with the hope of being a modern poem. Yet, sadly it was a failed one.

A rubber teat for my parents

According to my mother, I was circumcised by a heavenly host and was a very beautiful child before the typhoid fever got at me. This incident gave rise to new blood in my memory: in the Moullah (a primary school, where Muslim children must learn to recite the Koran by heart), I was unable to retain even the first lines of the holy Book. The mistress of the Moullah told my parents that I was a useless, brainless child and there was absolutely no need to send me to any school at all. My parents were convinced. Not feeling at ease seeing me staying at home at the age of eleven and being idle, they had to send me to a mixed primary school, which cost nothing all the same. At the end of the year, the Minister of Education awarded me the prize for being top of the form, which proved to be the case in the second year, the third and so on. Astounded, my family began to doubt the religious label imposed on me by the Moullah. At any rate, my family was elated about finally having such a brilliant child at home. They bestowed complete freedom upon me. My brothers and sisters received harsh punishment for any bad conduct they showed; sometimes their bodies were branded with red-hot skewers. I alone was pardoned, even if I had attempted to go along with adolescent hooligans to derelict sites, coupling with donkeys, cats and other things, which was the custom in Iraq. The reason behind forgiving me was, for them, an investment in the future. For years I became a subject to talk about. I remember that one day there was a heated discussion between my older brother and my father. Neither was able to read or write. According to my brother the best thing for me would be to study economics in the hope of becoming, for example, a Minister of Finance. For my father however, a better idea was to become a teacher, since there was more job-security than with a government post. Next door, I was reading Kafka's The Metamorphosis. I felt deep sorrow for

these poor people, seeing them build sandcastles in the wind. For, in as much as I started school late in life, I left it very early "from the most direct way possible: the window", as Harpo Marx so correctly put it. These poor people didn't get what the mistress of the Moullah meant when she said that I was a good-for-nothing. It was true that I was useless for Allah, the fatherland and the family.

Hence

The clock

The citizens of Konigsberg knew that it was exactly half past three when Immanuel Kant, in his grey coat, left his house and went to the lime tree avenue, so they are so precisely that the citizens set their watches behind him. The opposite prevails today: it is the philosopher who sets his watch by the masses and so he regulates his discourse according to the mechanics of the clock of the town. The philosopher's walk, as the citizens of Konigsberg called it, thus ended in a standstill.

Commitment

Once upon time, I had an appointment with a friend of mine, a one-eyed communist called Djabbar. I suggested seeing Doctor Caligari. He walked with me as far as the cinema and he didn't go in. He waited for me in a bar till the film had ended. When I came back, I told him that he had missed a good remake. He laughed about that, and said that I was brain-washed, and had to rinse my brain out. I didn't get what he meant by brain-washed. We walked together, me thinking there may be a chemist selling some potion to rinse our brains. We had done a lot of walking, always on our guard when, all of a sudden, we found ourselves in a front of the Russian Cultural Centre which was situated on the Abou Nowas riverbank in Bagdad, where they were giving a free show. He told me: "Here man, this is where you'll get your brain rinsed out". The idea appealed to me, so in we went. At the very moment the film started, a need to relieve myself came over me. I was stricken with diarrhea throughout the whole show.

On that day

In the distant past, on a boat moored to the flowery riverbank, while contemplating a sea bird clawing at the heights of Baghdad, I threw a few lines onto a paper that soon fell into the stream of my memory. At the riverbank, distant lands emerged thanks to a thread of imagination on which I clung to see the vast world, spying on the passing clouds.

So many lines, so many promises! They evaporated on the notebook of the dream. But the sky was so clear that I continued; writing and contemplating the sea bird crisscrossing the expanse of the rift.

Field of Stelae

Mute monoliths and rectangles of all heights, death moves among them with each ray of sunlight. Slabs of silence without any engraved memory, neither symbol, nor letter. The surrounding streets are the ones that keep the freshness of a language which melts the shadows escaping from old dates inscribed underground. In its darkness the no one's-rose still blooms...
Here is Reason, taking the bus to get off at the next station.
Not a single cloud nor the slightest assumption, alone in the arena.
And the sky projected her image on other horizons.

Academics, silhouettes with long necks, to whom comfort comes as a spark of memory and each of them eats under branches made of words. At the turn of the void, humor blazes like a street lamp. "Reality will not be conquered", cries a free poet obeying no precepts. No one will know that words will never be dressed by the pants of impossibility! At the fringes, there was a vastness scattered by strangers with dewy tears on their cheeks... there was a night lit by friends.
But now is a new day.

Life has an appointment in Berlin: to undress Enlightenment.

To be titled

I walk adrift
I notice a reformer lulling a society to change
I spot a tobacconist murdered by a cloud of smoke
I pounce on the shadow of Hans Anderson
      Plying truant
I skim through The Capital
I hear a revolutionary shouting behind bars
      I'll have another cup of revolution
      If you twist my arm.

I walk adrift
The whole day long
And before I sleep
I draw poets
Nibbling the sun's black teat.

Beneath veil

I remember how,
That day,
In the evening,
Your body comforted me.
I never saw you veilless,
It was spring,
The cold far from us,
The sun coating the beach
With a smile of old times
Its rays spread under the sheets!
The words clashed against the waves
While our lips ran
To quench their thirst
And our bodily souls
Bathed in fantasies,
Floated in the elliptical attraction of the depths!
I took a drink of your body, filling my lungs.
And the knowledge spills
Across the pages.
I think of you once more.
I see you lying on the sands that shine like starry skies!

I remember...
I feed on my memories of you
I drive through the folds of your absence
You are the appearance of all that illuminates.
Love has only one form: your body!
I loved you, I love you
And after all this

I will love you much more than before
No matter if love
Is nourished only by the delights of evil
And dies in monotony,
In the passionate tide of scandals!

The land of the poem

Another poet has left us. He went to the land of the poem,
one that we never read. He had mentioned it here and there in
indescribable sentences... He secretly worked on it all through his life.
One fine day we heard that he was about to finish. He flew with
joy, flew, flew higher, until he was hit by the absolute. Then he fell
dead like a bird hit by a hunter. Who knows! Perhaps he is now in
the land of the poem?
Normally, the poet - when he dies - has to wait a long time before
entering the land of the poem he promised us. In fact, he has
fooled us with this illusion.

Pay lip service

Everything is clarified.
But nothing is won.

In the battle of the mind,
The image, a thickness suspended
      From a shivering word,
Balances its new-found impatience
With its renouncement of identity,
On the surface of a manuscript,
Still in a liquid state.

Unpronounceable,
    It is its own shriek,
          Torn apart,
   Neither syllable
        Nor tracks,
Just a simple effigy.

Directions

Here I am in a bare garden.
A sound of water flowing in a relaxing solo.
Everyone practices sport in his own way.
The stems bloom in their beauty
     Driving sap between leaves and roots,
And like all ideas,
They are silent under the light
     And talkative in the dark.

Rays through a country in ruins

This morning the lungs of Baghdad are emptied of the lies of One Thousand and One Nights: no more magic carpets, no thieves or beggars becoming rich.

History, as far as the eye can see, vomits its events out onto the banks of the Tigris, where the timid sky is already washing all metaphors away with the whisky of the world. It is time for the city and the history to wash their laundry together.

White poem against no color

The Double has been revolutionized by Jean Benoît into a
necrophile, paranoid traits quicken his instances of a likeness
sedimented in the womb of the lens where the lip of id transpires
through the little moustache of the nervous one that Benoît has
doted upon in the gallery of the eye as the necrophile gleamed once
and for all to laugh back at The Double of Otto Rank.

Interbreeding

Neither rain, nor storm, nor all the waters of the world can fertilize
our tree. Unique of her kind, she remained sterile for a long time.
Only the northeast wind can push the pollen of a distant male
towards her pistils. And, thus, the people of my country are left
at the mercy of violent and cold winds.

Meridian

One day at noon, in ar-Rashid Street, I was devoured by hunger and without a penny. I saw a poet. I ran up to him and asked him if he could lend me some small change to buy a sandwich. He gave me a copy of his first collection of poems and said: "Eat!" I ate!

Profile of a man

He is a man
Who sleeps alone every night.
Who lives alone everyday
He dreams as he eats
He drinks as he shops
He opens his door to storms
The same way others slam their windows
       in the face of the night.

Here is a man
Who meets without doubt
The obligations of life!

Emulation

For Ladislav Guderna

Does the image eat
Does the word drink
Does the brush itself think.

On the fingertips
A shadow, a river
And moisture capable of giving birth
To living things.

Make money not love
Says the motto
And the oil rises up
In a pasture of thoughts
Breaking through the crust
To blink on the untrodden.

The image does not eat
The word does not drink
The brush does not think
But they keep hungering for a man
Benighted on the road
In the core of his eyes
      A blank on which
            The dream can finally rest.

Warm vision

A few steps
  Beyond
The white moon
 In the shape
Of a flaming eye,
  In the middle
Of a ruinous starlit night
Above the shade,
  Up there,
 A world,
    Grey,
     Shall die.

A simple change of address

The dead know nothing of their fate
They don't even know they are dead
And all that they have left,
Even if their glow still shines,
Remains inexorably doomed to decay,
                    Allegory, and dust.
Without even knowing that they are simply dead
They have sunk into an unknown blackness...
And as if they had never been born:
No memories
      No remorse
              No tears
Nor the slightest glimmer
To give them something to see
What they would have dreamed of achieving.

Exact lament

Another poet dies
Without listing those he hated.
If he had underlined with his contempt
All those names abhorred by poets
He would have disallowed,
        By one single poem,
Many baneful orations.

Poem

Moons
    Fragmented
        In a pond.

On the edge of the night
        Solitude
         Bleeds its legend.

Somnambule view

Looking down on the street from a roof, bristled with antennas,
My father
Said, wondering:
- The birds are gone!
In fact,
They had fallen asleep right above his head.

Cyclops' gaze

From a window,
    In the sun,
I take a long time
      In contemplating the world
                          Dismembered
On its bench.

Writing at all costs

For Reuven Snir

Dawn rises up over the mountain. Like one of these hens, the night's feathers ruffle and the owl blinks.

No one will wait for us. We have, like the old wise men in the answering villages, our eyes fixed on a falling star. We speak to each other lucidly. The whiteness of our eyes throwing a blind cry to the center of the earth. The morning after comes softly to our ears, like a huge yawn from the mouth of the horizon.

We are alone. The window is dim. A silhouette of metaphors watches over us.

We go through the night following the towers which, in the distance, succeed one another in order. We eat the flesh of the mists. A pouring rain surprises us, which pushes the silence to open its umbrella, to move towards the amphitheater. The moon splits. The sky drinks from the dusk and spits it into the gutters of the empty words.

Pubs summer time

From Victoria Station to Camden Town
From Camden Town to Notting Hill Gate
From Notting Hill Gate to Queensway
From Queensway adrift to Hyde Park
From Hyde Park to a woman's palm
From a woman's palm to the Buck's Head
From The Buck's Head to Leister Square
From Leister Square to a seat in the Night Owl.

Five days on an excursion
Yielded a big question mark
I lost it on the way back.

Organs without sex

What a Sunday, it was beautiful like a banana: the street was brimming over with vagabonds sooner or later disappearing in its dark corners; with bookshops whose shelves looked like vaginas ready to be despoiled; with pubs where drunks sometimes drool like soot drifting with galactic ejaculation.

Empty words

As the sun peeks over the horizon
In Baghdad everything flies away
Like all the magic carpets:
>   The blankets,
>   The sails,
>   The cables and flags,
>   The autumn leaves,
>   The odors,
>   The clouds,
>   The birds,
>   And all the girls' skirts!

Fruits

Tired of thrones,
The adolescent girl of Mesopotamia
Remained in the tower,
Spattered like a ripe thought.

In the foresight of the dawn
She tied the globe to her feet
And flew away from any bond.

Birth-line

For Gerald Stack

Towards the North of these lines
I make a step
Dreaming of the kinship
Broken into bones
At the bottom of the womb
Towards these lines
Of our beginnings
Nature creeps
Let the Sun lie down with the Moon
To dwell peaceably in its knitting
To throw daylight on a human theme
Towards these lines
Blasted off into blank
I wallow in clitoral flames
Bathed in the saliva
That first people had leaked out.

In the woods

Hand in hand,
On the road to San Romano,
The act of poetry, like love,
Binds us
    And leaves us swooning
        In an imperious figurative escape
That the copycats of the dawn of things,
Can in no way deflower
        Nor undo the sheets!

Birth

Sounding in my ear, the past suddenly invaded me and I found myself alighted on a fence. I started to look out over the first trace of the world: an alley, a stone and a scratched shadow on a façade. The king's procession is booed as it enters by birds of all colors, then applauded by a flock of crows. It was sunset. I opened the image's cage and flew away.

Design

On the dead-end road
The leaves of my destiny
      Hover like kites.
They crumble around a circle
Of light varnished with fog
Then break through a perspective
      Locked in the horizon.

Rupture

Fear not, a morning will come
When the beast will curl up.
Remember that;
    The trigger,
        The blood of your altars,
            And the belts of blue cartridges
Reside between your fangs.

Dive then
In the crepuscular tears
        Of your leaky stares
Until you find, scattered all over,
The calcined bones of your ancestors
And there you will have a place
      In the sun
         And a name
           On everyone's lips!

Infidelity

A world of disappointment.
    Disclosed by the word.

Cosmic
    In its fall,

Banal
    In its waking,

Always grows
    Against itself.

Desolation

Along houses
     Struck down
The windows intertwined infinitely,
The mind raises its flame
In front of these funeral-like ruins
        Snoring in the dark.

Sky

We go now to meet the eternal
With our beach stones
Under a birth sky
In an alley of mahogany and resurrection.
Outside, words cry for us,
Mixing salt with our emotions.
For centuries we have been howling in the void
In a castle of water and thorns.
We throw from time to time
Flocks of arrows at our hearts
Hanging from the ceiling
Because we are lovers without letters,
Without memories,
Mere stained-glass birds in flight.

Here we are, asleep in a cloister,
Its walls taunt
    The brood of the lammergeier
And the image crumbles around the bed!

Espionage

My country coughs in the bed
Under which the war is relegated
      Like an old sock.
My idle hands
Have been incubating a project for ages
I am a spy,
A paid agent of words,
I hide behind the brackets,
Between the ramifications of meaning.
I spend my holidays at the beach
      Playing dice
With punctuation marks and references.
I touch the light on the water.
    It vibrates among pebbles,
The waves lead me astray.
And as soon as I return to my bed
    My country bursts
Pus-like, all over the universe.

Illusions of the desert

The journey is so long,
That the traces fade day after day,
The curves sag,
Having altitude without consequences!
The desert, the first day of transparency!
No dune interrupts the horizon.
The immensity is always in its own clothes.
The day eclipses the stars.
Nothingness is the only building
That can rise on the sand!
The desert sees no further than the end of its dunes!
No dream,
    No asphalt meadow
        No millennium grasses.
It is a world buried in the sight,
        A sudden and uncoupled time.
The desert, an hourglass of infinity,
Tatters of nowhere,
Towards which the word gravitates!

Low ground

In the distance,
      The swell is calming in the blue.

Closer to me,
A dune spreads out
      With curves so fine
        And incandescent
That the phantoms of the first apparition
Disappeared into it without even being seen.

Thought bubbles in the void!

I wonder what Franklin Rosemont would have done

The wind waved the clock hands of the city
Where the birds are transfigured
Into courtesan's handkerchiefs.

The black swan
Left us for other lakes!
The skyscrapers are translucent
The books are available in display racks
Under the rays of a cursed halo.

It was a Sunday
Drawn in watermark
On the imaginary notebook of his last trip!

The battle will be long
To erase the frail comma
That separates
        The portrait from the analogy,
                The banal from the sublime!

Poor Death!

Death does not drink!
He doesn't believe in omens
Nor in flames.

>Behind his curtain
>Dust gazes at his own reflection.

Always severe, death remains
A prisoner of his own whiteness,
When around the horizon
He picks up someone
On a wagon with chimeras!
Death solitaire,
Alone with his greasy smells of corridors,
Like a tavern
Where the world emerges...
And time plays tricks on us!

The poets' kiss

Being as one with the familiar saliva,
The poets' kiss,
That sweet rustle of the lips,
Makes the tongue sing
So that the senses are awakened
And in the mouth melts *the amber,*
   The musk, the benzoin, incense
And all these perfumes flowing from the unknown!

In the valleys and hills of the body,
The kiss of the poets makes the fur
Bristle and the zephyr whisper
Before imprinting such a memory,
The furtive trace of its enjoyment,
On the cheeks of the book!

The kiss of the poets,
As long as the lips are wet,
As long as the words are erogenous.

The death of the ego

In this chamber of consolation
Courage has no beak,
Nor the face, teeth.

The remnants of the divine image
Make the consciousness imperfect,
A neck-tie that the word
      Can wear
            During the butterflies' ball.

The hour of the poem

The tree of life
Gives the sentimental skyscrapers a sign.
Its fountain-like leaves
Follow one after another,
Each meridian carrying
To the ramparts of the tree of science
The log-book of the garden of Eden
To pay for the mistake
By sharing with the shadows
    The ashes of light!

Human, too human

Meanwhile, Baghdad is far away.

I was thirteen years old, when I used to accompany my father several mornings a week to help him open his little tea stall in a major fish market on the banks of the Tigris. When we arrived that winter morning, we saw regular customers and passers-by were crowding near the bank, "Poor Abbas", we could hear. A grey mist was flowing from the sky. The dead body of the fishmonger had just been discovered lying in his little boat. White foam was coming out of his mouth, he was holding a bottle of alcohol in his hand and around him were, still wriggling, a few fish he had caught before his strange death. What had he died of? No one could tell. However, the night was cold and Abbas was known as an insatiable drinker. I still remember his big Nietzschean moustache, but Abbas knew nothing of the philosopher. He was a simple man; his life had been devoted to casting his net in the vivid water to the extent that the only good fish he caught each day had become his only opinions. His death caused a great stir that day.

A flight of fancy

When I rode the mount of a dead knight,
There were processions of clouds above my head.
Pure streams, caves and valleys at my door,
And under my feet the thrill of the hills.
What a beautiful illusion!
      Dancing in ecstasy,
            Opening the doors of the world
And seeing the moon crack.

The spirit of words

United by the cold,
The tree, the bird, the clouds
Suffer from the same wounds of absence
            As the idea,
    That troubled foam of the brain,
Which rushes
    Towards unstrung risk
                And bends over
On its robe of water.

The passenger

I sway between two paradises
      In a double dream,
The sun lies on the world's treacherous bed.
I wait for a wink from eternity,
Its voice is running through my ear.
Light and wine,
Stag and pepper!
Darkness like the green fairy turns to emotion.
The night like intriguing surf
Melts drop by drop
Into mental tides
Palacing the landscape.

Being inside so long,
I have not slept since the conquest.
No dawn in the desert skies
No song, no bell,
The camels show only the dunes.
No camel driver to lead them in chanting;
Only thunder-winged twilights.

Hell contemplates the world from its starry window
The sense flees the dead smell, like that of geranium,
I free the sparrow from my fingertips.
The skeletal past starts to dance
And the angels, near earth, organize themselves
To illuminate the sky of the muse!

Virginity of passage

Everything shines in dryness,
In inexorable determination to disappear...
We suffocate under the pavement of our pores.
The understanding bends each ray.
The perspective, as a distant mirage
Lounges in our eyes,
      And warms the languor.

The spirits are winning us over.
The call of the bush
    Haunts our forms
From root to root.

Flames and banners clatter
Above the void
    Under a pre-diluvian breath,
A wet branch as a kind of offering.

Writing, riding

I journey with words
As a Bedouin with his camels
Grazing cattle of senses
Through endless sheets,
Under a setting sun
For beauty rejuvenation.

End of winter

Snow-covered
And sad of whiteness,
The world still sleeps in the pool of time
Like a sunflower without shelter.

Childhood cries under a fir tree,
The house is lit with absence,
While the sleeper
Abandoning the standing walls,
Inclines in his crystal dreams.

On the roof of the phenomena
The future gives birth to another present
And the metaphors accumulate on our shoulders.

Language dwelling

For Amir Or

The ochre-colored house of the being is alone in plain, its rooms
lead one into another. It is located in one of the serpentine
meanings, on the steps of vocables, fog and sloping shadows. The
ideas, covered with the soot of dreams, row along the enclosure,
forming with it one unit in the hall of eloquence:
How strange this singing from within,
      These lighthouses,
        This quiddity,
          And that bird above the plain...
As if they were never seen!

It is a house constant as memory.
Illuminated by a silent constellation, its stare marvels at all the
beasts of the earth.

The southern noon

Your listening ears,
Your watchful eyes,
Are no longer, merely indulgent organs.
They belong to the past footsteps
And the present limestones
that glitter when day breaks like a new born.

No poetry wants you
Your frenzy wanders with you.
Silt along unknown shores
Gives evidence.
A rope between you and your double
Unravels in the open sea.
The slime of a new sun
Flows down the roofs
Of your flaky life!
Your skin remains dazed with memories,
Your alchemy knocks around in time
And in the freshness of the streams,
From the visual to the verbal,
Your guts spilled
Destined to splash
In your own home.

Leave nothing of you in you
And your fears ripen into beams of light
Broken across the eyeshadows.
This is your last morning:
The second coming
          Of the poem!

Secular mysticism

Lying on the ground
Under a yawning horizon,
My soul has forgotten
        For hours
That it was there!

Lines in the spectrum

I only have my dreams,
Hung on the walls of a mountain
That no valley can hold,
Rescued from a night isolated in time
And laced to the edge of the universe.

I only have stories full of ideas,
Unknown to turntables
If I put two of my fingers
On an upturned glass
And dialogue with idle-minds:
Melancholy first
Then a salve for the eyelashes,
Blinking,
Like the advertisement above the entrance door.

I only have a bed of words
Where poetry can be prescribed in doses.
Nice to see herein blue dance
When the images blossom
And give to closed phrases,
        Rites and arguments!

I have only one divided life:
Meaningless to the breath of the ephemeral,
And the other, posthumous,
Lying in the ruins of eternity.

How to be very close and very far at once
While my dreams never repeat themselves
And my memory takes a shower
After each exhale.

The dialectic goes up in the air

Nothingness, man and the word
Three points in one line, expected by existence.
Deliverance, with a swollen chest, brings them
To the narrative
   Under the flame of the lamps,
Where the spirits keep dark,
Protected by plants rinsed with mystery.

They spend their time,
Like a key outside a lock,
      Tying ribbons to laces,
Looking for an idea
Which snuggles up against them.
Once the first glimmer appears
Here they are overwhelmed in the details.

Half shadow

Wherever the night lightens,
The certainty of light
Bumps into a stump of shadow.
The sky opens its belly to dust
Splashed onto objects of desire
As if Day, wounded by a rainbow,
Wants to marry Lady Darkness,
Putting an end to a common fear,
Chiseled like a wordless rock.

The poets

Under the moon just after sunset,
They have quenched their thirst
And wrapped their forbidden silhouettes
      In the great book of pictures.

*A*rt *S*et *I*n *D*ynamic *E*mulation

For Tony Pusey

Lend your ears not to gossip,
but to your inner calls
Give the sun a chance to lift
A robe of night
Playful Jinn is in town
with jars of wine
And camel's milk
Let the brush, your mind's prudent-sister,
Ache to bear.

There are times
When it is better to be a drifter
Than to be set in a mission
Times when you realize in advance
Whatever you do is bound to become
A circular letter
A spider's trace, tangents of impotence:
Prism of being there.

Like an insect simulating leaves
Mind constitutes forms that can shape it up.

What an anonymity it is to conceive
Flashes in a crystal dark
Horizons off stage, a landscape of motion-sounds?

Postulates are a cessation of growth.

Lend, give, let
And slide away.

The image while it mushrooms,
Rebels for the fit
Between the eye and the seen.

Thinking is a line.

Alchemy

It is a dark feeling with the blank stare
Which creeps into me right now
Years on
Nothing resounded
On the contrary
The whole seems to succumb
To the white night's mercy of darkness
Whose mouth has long since been watering
For a bit of light
I pick up a book
I start to read
At such hour of modern times
Sparks of serenades
Old serenades
Are struck from my grasshopper mind
I glimpse pleasant memories
Buzzing like bees delivered from reflexive waters
They knock me down with a feather
Everything is dark
The navel, the star,
The little idea of the world
That Enlightenment has pierced in us
And the field of research
For the way out.
Even our socks smell dark.
Look at that roof,
Bathing in a blond haze
Is the dark, laying in ambush for it
Yet we lie, kill, defeat
Love, write
And make no leaps in the dark.

Language irregularities

For Roger Cardinal

Nouns to verb
Teen-agers to nipple
Heart-woods to river
Phrases to somehow
Horizons to image
Daylights to evening
And countless dreams to indeed.

Sometimes, herewith

For Marianne Ivsic

No title.
No date.
No signature.
A painting is a sun-dial.
History a dark horse.
Everything is an outline.
Career is our scar.

It is the foot
Not the floor
Which pin-points the ceiling of the voyage.
It is the eye not the hand
Which holds the microcosm
Of what flickers at each sight.
It is Charles Fourier
Emerging in letter and spirit
Who looms large at night.
It is those virginal times,
Blind alleys of our daily life.
It is the inside of the whole
Where silence narrates.
It is this and that,
Explosive consonant,
Nostalgia?
A state of mind.

The celebration day of my childhood

When the sun reclines along the shoulder of the night
When the people drink their remembrance
And disappear in a faucet
When the outcry of an injured cloud honks the town
When solitude goes foundering between my hands
When the roar of the seer leaks out of my door
When the mouth swallows the Word with a glass of haze
When the dream makes a mess of the sea
When my laughter wanders in despair near your table
When eyesight swarms the void with labyrinth
When boredom falls to decay
And the moment rises up voyaging in a timeless region
I will plunge in there
Bringing you here
And balancing my childhood on your absence
Like a bald light
On a distance of ice.

When the star eats a black sky

For Ted Joans

A lurid mermaid prevails on my exuberant circulation of spume
muddied with the blood of sleep that chains the herd of hands
already released from the sore throat of dust where the audible hats
flying like ravens in the light of caution whose air murmurs in the
tranquility of lightning as a signal of the revolt of the neighing in a
society for the prevention of cruelty to hands.
For laziness has a revolutionary function:
The game stalks the moment.

Under the skin

Cradle of gazes addressing the horizons
Cradle of fingers on trigger
Cradle of myths preparing the book
> Of cemeteries without graves
> Of unspeakable silence
> Of ghostly notebooks
> Of wars and plants
> Of grey zones
> Of present absences
> Of time without assassins
> Of wings and feathers
> Of metal herbs
> Of ghosts dancing in the void
> Of double and mirror
> Of counter-currents of the self
> Of mechanical clouds
> Of rhizomes at the roots of speech.

Cradle of action and interference
Where death and life meet
> Adrift
> > In the whirlwind
> > > To come!

Everything is with a fluid of questions

Toward this North
     Thrown in a breach
I take a step
Dreaming of fragmented kinship
     At the bottom of the womb.

The beginning
Remains unchanged
     Meek and tangled!

The dog-tired dogs

In the dog days
I witnessed a dogfight
Between top dog
And underdog
Who were dogged by misfortune,
By a life gone to the dogs.

In the dog days
I saw the gay dog
Whose liquid eyes are tight-lipped
Lashing a horse
Like a yellow rain slashing a linotype.

In a dog's life
Always
Nostalgia remembered.

For after all
Why should one let sleeping dogs lie?

Words eat raw

… Even now, I try to make sure this attempt was successful. Without it though, the streams of reflection would have been lost.

The poem stumbles in front of this sudden deadlock which never closes its eyelids. It consciously follows a thought, un occult amalgam of language, that clashes with its own hallucinated discoveries. A fleeting enjoyment. I began to bang against the walls of the unconscious, so violently that blood spurted from my head. At that moment my mouth became the crater of my thoughts. Words came out recklessly, piercing the sheets piled before me: dissolute vocables, odorless. I cannot underestimate the effusion. It appears to me as a scene crossed by a prophesy, surfaced by the illusion of seeing the very act of writing. The sheets are being sucked into a maelstrom of what was going on in my head. Notes scribbled here and there. I hear their whistle. I contain their wheat. Each paragraph is an orchard and the meaning a resting place.

My thought, reflection of a being hidden in the depths of time, appears in this moment of creation, as the groaning expression of a sensory experience that rises and falls.

Everything passes through and participates in the immensity of space: the place, the time, the houses, the elements… So many secrets remained buried under the meaning, unseen to the eye of modernity. Yet, aged secrets are as empty of significance as the orbits of the dead, pale objects that soon crumble under the shock of revelation and unrealized consequences. At the lightning's calm, the sleeping world whizzes. To write is to shatter the closed window of the internal. It is to launch a cry and run into the night.

Yes, the image will come one day, and we will make love on a bed of clouds and clays. Stick to your obsessions and to your breath, the rhythm inside you. Another truth, energetic, will rise from the nostrils of the immediate!

Poetry, the oxygen of man, its desires can be satiated by its mediums, the words, when they reclaim their right to run freely through the threads, roses and chains… Words consistently state what they convey. Automatic revelation. Human beings live by words. In fact, we are alive only within words. Only words remember us. The ego is part of the word, and their framework is speech. We utter words before they give us tongue…; to such a degree, that we make them hollow like the void where everything gets buried and forgotten. The forgotten, this deluding *unmastered past*, does not die out. It always peers through each breath, each image like a returning ghost. It is necessary to work the stone of the image.

I like words bristling with the dewclaws of a fierce rooster. They sound like rain, release lightning in the heart of darkness. They raise the magnitude of the contemporary man, reviving, from all directions, his imagination and set him in revolt. While exchanging confidences in celebration of the ephemeral, words like cats, escape from the cage of the lexicon… and stray away into the unknown.

Rise up narration, get involved in the riot of words where the lips get wet.

Reality is a beast that walks cautiously on the wastelands of survival. It cannot return to itself without a swig of utopia, a shiver that runs through the realm of necessity.

I see, from a suspended boat, trembling shores.

A hat whitens foolishly and flies into the void.

I kick the names of the past.

I chose life.

From afar, it seems that a blaze awakens with a slap of flame the exact image.

The first ovules surge, leaving sleep. They communicate to us what their compeers, the poets, were simmering. Thought do not always lose sight of language. It braves the memory.

Here is the syntax unmasking the face of the grammar.

Here is the bird of ambivalence in search of a protective doubt.

Hither and thither the effusion…

Word is Other within each of us. The dream, it tells, unites us.

To avoid confrontation and feel the truth being born in your mouth, all you'll need is to awaken the gang of mirrors.

Poems are not Pavlovian dogs, aesthetic salivation, but mental explosives to blow all the walls. Drink from the poets' vessels, and you will feel their light bursting upon you.

The dawn, always standing, falls in pieces like a memory ready to confess and to unload its bag; landscapes, horizons, and ruins flying on the sheets.

The poem points to the ultimate debacle at the door of the poet.

Writing is digging through the wall of language to catch a glimpse of the secret life of the word.

— July 2022

Acknowledgements

They will be back before the light: It often happens, when writing a poem, certain lines that one has read in the past, impose themselves on the mind to the point of becoming part of the text to come. This poem bears witness to these reminiscences. The reader will thus recognize the luminous and fleeting presence of Baudelaire, Breton, Crane, Kunitz, Levertov, Stevens, Pound... whose lines are indicated in italics. Special thanks to William Stephenson and Michael Richardson for their proof reading.

The whole book is translated from Arabic and French by the author.

LAY OUT YOUR UNREST